HOW TO BECOME AN EMCEE

HOW TO BECOME AN EMCEE

Everything you need to know to turn your passion

into a paycheck

DHWANI RAO

To my family and all the event organizers I've worked with.

Thank you for the opportunities.

CONTENTS

BONUS

"The future has many names: For the weak, it means the unattainable. For the fearful, it means the unknown. For the courageous, it means opportunity."

— *Victor Hugo*

Introduction

It was the summer of 2007. I had just graduated from high school and it would be four months before I started college. I was an enthusiastic and ambitious seventeen-year-old. It was my most memorable summer because that year I was able to turn my passion into something that paid, and which eventually became my career.

A friend introduced me to the exciting world of events, which was just emerging. For some pocket money, I worked jobs like distributing pamphlets in a crowded mall, awkwardly standing next to a life-size shampoo display in a supermarket, lending my voice to a cartoon character on a TV show, being an extra in an Indian feature film, and helping event organizers backstage at live events.

I was captivated by the glamour of showbiz. At these events, I watched and observed the emcees and thought that I could do this too. I accompanied a friend who was auditioning for an event to become its emcee. When we got to the office she got cold feet and nervous, and I stepped up and asked the organizer if I could audition instead. I landed my first event.

I went back to the crowded mall, this time as an emcee. I loved the power and the adrenaline rush that came with being under the spotlight, holding a mic, hearing my voice projected loud on the speakers around me, and having hundreds of people watching me and listening to what I was saying. I was addicted and there was no going back. Being an emcee gave me an identity, and made me feel special; I immensely valued myself. As a result of this, I became a more confident person. Only as an adult, I realize how important it is that everybody gets to feel this way about themself. Becoming an emcee is the best decision I have made in my life. My life changed over the course of one sensational summer.

I didn't just get lucky. I worked hard for it. I went to college five days a week pursuing an engineering degree, and over the weekends hosted day-long product promotional events in crowded places. Back then most of the emcees were television and radio personalities. I was neither and nobody knew me. I networked hard and did not turn down a single event because

I was tired. I knew all the nine hour long events and my hard work would eventually reward me. And they did. I would hear about other popular emcees and how much their pay check was and dreamt of getting paid the same. Years later, when it finally happened, it felt so surreal.

If you wish to become an emcee, it doesn't matter which profession you are currently in, your educational qualifications, how old you are, and certainly not your gender. You could be in school, taking a sabbatical from work, raising kids, or perhaps just looking at it as a "side hustle". You should and must give yourself an opportunity to turn your hobby into something that pays.

There is also no age restriction for being an emcee. Colleagues whom I look up to are in their forties and fifties. The event industry is massive and its needs diverse. There is a place for you. This profession is for those who can hold their own, have a personality, exhibit presence of mind, and can think on their feet, as well as be able to say the right things at the right time.

Throughout this book, I will share insights from my experience as a corporate emcee and event host of eleven years, and what I learned after hosting about 1000 events for hundreds of international brands and corporations. It took me several mistakes and failures to understand the intricacies of being an emcee. So I want to help shorten your learning curve, saving you embarrassment by sharing the right way to handle everything involved with hosting an event. I wish there had been a handbook with guidelines when I started my career as an emcee. I hope you make the best of this book and enjoy my insights on getting started, preparing for your show, managing glitches, dealing with stage fear and nervousness, and executing an event onstage. This book will also dive into the business aspect of this profession, tell you what your potential clients are looking for, fee negotiation, and how to create a "hot" personal brand.

When starting something new, it's only natural to have doubts and questions in your mind about your capabilities. You have to fight these voices in your head. The only way to quieten these doubts is to be patient with yourself, prepare, practice well, get rejected a few times, and make the best of every opportunity you get to be an event host.

Lastly, give yourself permission to be a beginner. There is honor in working hard, practicing and learning from mistakes, but your persistence is key. In following your passion, you are opening up to new experiences and putting yourself out there, in front of hundreds of people. Being out of your comfort zone is scary, but this will help you grow and create a newer version of yourself that you will truly be proud of.

Writing this book has been therapy on steroids. It has given me the opportunity to reflect on my work, growing as an emcee, and all that I have learned through this journey. I am so humbled by the experience of putting together this book and honored to share it with you. As you step into the extraordinary world of events, I wish you truly experience all the joys of being onstage and bringing events to life. I hope this book brings you all the success you deserve.

1.

How can you enter this profession?

"All our dreams can come true— if we have the courage to pursue them."

—*Walt Disney*
Entrepreneur

I started my career hosting birthday parties for kids, promoting brands at malls, schools, and office cafeterias before venturing further into corporate events and business conferences. All the opportunities I had onstage and in front of the microphone made me a better emcee and prepared me for the big events that followed. The experience also helped me make industry connections and led me to meet the amazing people who gave me bigger opportunities to showcase myself.

A great way to start your career is to get some experience and practice onstage. Take any opportunity you can—an event at your college, your friend's baby shower, a fundraiser, charity event, or even an office get-together.

If you are a student, be part of the groups and organizations within your college or school and be cognizant of what events are coming up. At the nascent stage of such events, use this window of opportunity to put in a word with the organizing team about your inclination to help host a show. Doing this early will give the committees that are involved the time and bandwidth to make a decision. By being part of the organizing team, you can observe the planning process that supports the entire event onstage and backstage. Even if you don't get to be the emcee, brainstorm and work with the host on the script and show flow, amongst other logistics.

A similar approach can be taken if you work at an office. Volunteer to host office events. You may also want to speak to the HR representatives, or whoever is in charge, to inform them that you would like to host some of the activities planned. An advantage is that you are hosting in front of your colleagues and work friends so their feedback will be honest. Also, since you are volunteering, there is less pressure on you. You will get away with small blips because you are doing it out of an interest to entertain, and you might even have your friends and seniors motivate you.

Another option is when you hear of a friend's upcoming baby shower. You can also use that opportunity to volunteer to be the emcee and get some crucial on-the-job training. A good starting point might be to take up the task of organizing activities and games for the mommy-to-be's friends. In addition to doing something helpful for a friend, you'll also get the bonus of receiving valuable feedback from people who will be honest and candid.

Join clubs, groups, and local communities, and volunteer for their events. Be there at all the meetings and help in planning the events, and volunteer to be the emcee at them. This is a perfect platform to be seen and let everyone know your skill. People will notice your good work and might get in touch with you the next time they require an emcee.

I advise you to not practice your hosting skills on a paid gig too soon, as it's stressful to hone your skill this way. And the responsibility for the success of the entire show is on the event organizer. If your paid gig is your first time hosting an event onstage, then it is important to be honest with the event organizer about it. Let them assess your capability and make a decision as to whether they are comfortable having you as their host.

How can you look for gigs?

Once you have some experience hosting a few events, leverage this to find paid gigs. It is time to let your friends and family, and all those in your network, know about your new side hustle.

Update on social media

Tell the world that YOU CAN EMCEE! To begin with, add a prefix or title, 'Emcee' or 'MC', to your name on Facebook, Instagram, and Twitter. Adding this title is the easiest way to convey to your network that you are open for business. Change your profile photo to a picture of you speaking onstage.

Find the right people using social media

A path forward in your new journey would be to utilize social media, such as Facebook and LinkedIn, to find event organizers in your city and to send them a connection request with a short and interesting introduction of yourself. The message should convey that you are a burgeoning emcee and would like to connect with him/her. Also, you might consider reaching out to other emcees, your counterparts, and the people you look up to within this industry. Add them to your online social network. By doing this, you have started the first steps in attaining the relevant audience for all your event-related social media updates, and created a channel for people to get in touch with you when they have a requirement.

Document your work

Get a friend or a professional photographer to capture photos of you hosting an event onstage. Collect testimonials from clients and organizers who appreciate your performance. These can be used in your emcee profile and website.

Create an Emcee Profile

An emcee profile is what a portfolio is to a model—the conduit that allows you to showcase your talent to event managers. This is a useful tool to email to organizers when they get in touch with you. My first emcee profile was a collection of photos of me, the type of events I had hosted, names of the companies I had worked with, and concluded with my contact details. It was all in a vibrant and upbeat PowerPoint presentation.

Fast forward to the present: I have outgrown the animation, slide transition effects, and my lengthy presentation of eighteen slides. My current profile is a PDF document with a few images of me from my recent events, a short paragraph about my strengths as a show host, a list of my most popular clients, and links taking the viewer to my videos on YouTube. It is all within six sheets.

Don't try to fill the profile with too much information. Keep it brief and keep the presentation short. Since the profile is sent on email or shared on Whatsapp it is often viewed on a mobile device. So make sure the file size is not too big and the profile is easy to download.

If you are a beginner or have to work with minimal resources, I suggest you make a PowerPoint presentation with details about yourself and the work you have done so far. Put together your best onstage shots, add information about the various types of events you have done, and name the companies you've hosted events for.

If you have done a substantial number of events, or you think you have too much content to fit into one profile, you can create multiple profiles. Create a profile highlighting your expertise in hosting conferences. Create another for family events like weddings and birthday parties. So when an organizer gets in touch with you for a business conference, you can send them our specific profile containing details of your experience and competency in hosting conferences.

Get the word out

Speak to a few friends, family members, and well-wishers about becoming an emcee and ask if they know anybody in the events industry in your city such as event managers, conference organizers, wedding planners, or even artist managers. Request them to introduce you via an email or on the phone. Also, ask your friends and family if they know someone who is getting married or hosting an event and if they might need an emcee.

Having a mentor

Reach out to fellow emcees and hosts in your area and ask if you can be an apprentice, as some accomplished emcees might be willing to mentor you. Seasoned emcees don't take up every event inquiry they receive. When they turn down an event, given their potential reputation, they might suggest another competent emcee. This way, a mentor can guide and groom you and, most importantly, help you find work with reputed organizers.

Hire an artist manager

An artist manager can also help you land gigs by pitching your emcee services to relevant contacts. They may be able to share insights into the industry and connect you with the right opportunities. You will need to share a percentage of your fee with the artist manager for every gig they get you. Another option is to work on a retainer model, where you pay a fixed monthly fee to your manager to get you gigs. Work on a format that suits you best. Similarly, there are platforms online for event artists where you can list yourself and upload your images and contact details. This way you are opening more avenues for prospective clients to get in touch with you.

Network

Be seen. Attend industry events and meet-ups. Find out if there is a local community of event organizers or event professionals in your city. Reach out to the organizer of the meet-ups and use this as a platform to network with professionals. Make your presence known there and introduce yourself.

2.

How do you prepare to be an emcee

"It usually takes me more than three weeks to prepare a good impromptu speech."

– Mark Twain
Writer

When I landed my first gig, I spoke to a professional emcee I knew, asking for guidelines and tips on how to prepare. Unfortunately, all I got was some wishy-washy advice like "just go up there and be yourself", which is simply not true!. Emceeing and hosting shows is beyond "being yourself". It is about the brand, the event's goal, the audience, and it takes significant preparation and practice. Be very wary of anyone who, without context, just says "be yourself". It's the laziest advice to give somebody.

There is an incredible amount of work that goes on backstage before the spotlight shines onstage. A good emcee is someone who uses the resources given and packages them to enhance the experience of their audience.

Understanding the event

It's imperative as an emcee to have clarity and information on key aspects of your event. Here are some questions you need to ask your organizer/client.

- What is the purpose of the event?
- What are we celebrating?
- Who is your audience?
- Is there a theme for the event?
- What are the highlights or ideas that need to be re-iterated through the show?
- Does the event aim to motivate, impart knowledge, get more sales, or unwind and party?
- What is the agenda of the event?

Having a clear understanding of the premise is very important, as you are the face of the event and the show runner onstage. You are representing the event on behalf of the organizers. The event's success depends on your skill of methodically navigating the audience through the entire show and making it seamless.

Understanding the audience

Your audience could be the top management of a corporation, employees of a company, or family of the host. The event is about them.

Understanding the profile of your audience and the expected number of attendees will help you prepare how to present yourself onstage. There is a significant difference in hosting a business meeting for an audience of thirty versus hosting an annual bash for a group of 500 employees of a company. Knowing about the audience in advance will help you plan the style and tone you want to set. If your hosting style has a lot of humor and wit, this knowledge will help you avoid jokes that are likely to make the guests uncomfortable.

If the event requires you to conduct games as fillers, knowing the age group, profile, and headcount of the attendees will help in planning appropriate ones.

Knowing what to say

To prepare my script and the crucial message in my opening, I ask my organizer a simple question: What do you want me to convey when I welcome the audience? Jot down all the points they want you to incorporate. Take the information you have, enhance it, and make it lively and compelling. This exercise of simply asking what should be said in the opening actually allows you to understand their goal better and removes any miscommunication between you and the organizer who has a certain vision for the event.

Understand the flow of events. You need to have a copy of the agenda on you at all times on the day of the event. We have come a long way with technology and teleprompters, but having the event schedule on paper, and with you, is still the most reliable option. I have noticed some emcees read their script or refer to the agenda on their phone when hosting onstage. Using a phone as a cue card makes the host seem unprofessional and sluggish.

Once the organizer has created and approved the event agenda, get yourself a copy. Make sure copies of the agenda are given to the team at the audio-video console, the backstage managers, and the event managers. This is to make sure everybody working on the event is on the same page and on track at all times.

Prepare your communication, your opening, and what you will say during the show. Organize your thoughts. Put your script on paper. In a later chapter, I explain in detail about what goes in your script. I have also included sample scripts you can use.

Make notes and create a framework for your script. Put down keywords or hints you can refer to. Should you invite a speaker onstage, practice pronouncing their name. If the name is difficult for you to pronounce, check with the organizer or the speaker as to the right way to pronounce the name. If there are any entertainment performances scheduled, prepare a script to describe and introduce the act and its performers.

Practice

There is no such thing as too much practice. Practice what you plan to speak onstage. Keep reading your script over and over again till the keywords and names comfortably roll off your tongue. Stand up and speak out loud while practicing the script. While rehearsing, check the tone you are using. If you notice you are speaking too fast, get used to slowing down, and identify where you would like to pause. Use your phone to make an audio recording of yourself reading the script. Replay and listen to the audio recording and let the content register in your mind. Correct your pitch, tone, and speed as required.

Arrive at least an hour before show time. Request the organizers for a dry run onstage before the audience arrive.

Audience engagement

The best way to make an event lively is by getting your audience to take part and be involved in the celebration. However formal or casual the event setting, audience engagement can go a long way in creating delight. Depending on the kind of event you are hosting and the profile of the members in the audience, plan your ice-breakers. My favorite kind of audience engagement is to walk among them, start a conversation, and get them to sing or dance. Have a few sure-fire audience engagement ideas that you can pull-off at short notice.

Videotape your performance and get feedback

Get a friend to videotape your portion of the event. Watch it. How do you sound? How do you look? Notice the mistakes you make. Are you pacing too much onstage or are you speaking too fast? Are you using too many crutch words like 'umms' and 'aahs'? Are you loud enough? Check your posture and body language onstage. Get feedback and make the necessary changes. Continue learning and working on yourself. When I look at a few event videos of mine, I can instantly tell you if at any point I was feeling extra nervous because I pace and move a lot when I'm nervous. This is something I never realized until I watched my videos. And I have since begun working on correcting and focusing my movement onstage.

Make peace with the fact that mistakes will happen. Be prepared and ready to own up to the mistakes and handle them with grace. That is what truly matters. If you make a mistake onstage, apologize for it and correct yourself. If you wrongly pronounce a speaker's name, apologize to them after the event. Know that the biggest and most common mistakes are the ones that happen before you speak, like not smiling when you welcome the audience, not having the right posture,

21

lacking eye contact, or not sounding enthusiastic when hosting. So work equally on the verbal and non-verbal aspects of emceeing while preparing for your event.

3.

What do you do after getting an event?

"One important key to success is self-confidence. An important key to self-confidence is preparation."

— *Arthur Ashe*

American tennis player

When looking for an emcee, organizers shortlist a few and call or email them to check on their availability and their remuneration for hosting. The organizing team compares emcee profiles and their fee. A few calls back and forth later, the organizers finalize on one emcee. Every time I get booked for an event, I have closed a deal. I take a moment to enjoy this tiny victory before a whole lot of preparation and planning begins.

Once you receive a confirmation for an event, block the date and time on your calendar to avoid college schedule or day job from overlapping.

Request the event organizer send you an email confirmation. This email should state that the organizing company confirms you for your services as an emcee for the particular date. Draw up a contract. This is to make sure things are structured and on paper. Create an invoice, to get your payment processed. The invoice should contain

- Your name
- Contact information (address, phone number, email ID)
- Invoice number
- Details of the company you are billing towards
- Event details
- Your fee (tax related details if applicable)
- Details of how the payment should be made (depends on your country)
- Your signature

Next, speak to the organizers or meet with them to discuss the event. Here are some details you must know to help you prepare.

- ✓ What type of event is it? What is the occasion?
  Is it a fun evening, a celebration, or a formal award ceremony?
- ✓ Who is your client and what do they do?
  Look on the internet for information about the client company and what it does. Details of recent achievements will give you an edge, both during your personal interaction with the client's team and during the show
- ✓ Know your audience
  What is the average age group of the audience? Are the attendees employees of the company? Are they customers of your client? Knowing your audience will help you plan how to present yourself and how to draft a script that is relevant to them.
- ✓ What is the expected turnout for the event?
  Is it an intimate gathering or are you hosting a show for 4000 people in the audience?
- ✓ Information on the logistics
  The event venue, timings, etc. If the venue is out of

your city, discuss your travel and accommodation arrangements. All travel expenses are covered by the organizer.

✓ You need to ask your organizer for a copy of the event schedule or flow of events.

✓ Names and designation of the key players

✓ What is your dress code? Is there a theme for the event?

Decide what you will be wearing. If you are renting a special occasion dress or thematic attire, plan it ahead of time, so it is in place and with you for the day. If you would like to use a professional's help with your makeup and hair, get an appointment booked for the date.

✓ If you are interviewing speakers onstage, do quick research about them and prepare the questions you are going to ask.

✓ If you are conducting crowd engagement through fillers or games, procure all the props required.

✓ If there is a script that the organizers have prepared, read it over multiple times and get familiar with the major points you have to emphasis through the event. Practice your spiel and rehearse.

- ✓ If you are not given a script, make one. Send it to the organizers and get it approved.
- ✓ Get a good night's rest. Proper sleep is very underrated. I need my eight hours of sleep to be my best onstage.

4.

Overcome stage fear and nervousness

"Best way to conquer stage fright is to know what you're talking about."

— Michael H Mescon
Author

Public speaking is infamously ranked as the number-one fear among Americans. The statistic says people fear public speaking more than they fear death and snakes. This is the most misinterpreted statistic that has been popularised by gatekeepers to discourage the general public from pursuing public speaking.

We do not fear public speaking. What we fear is 100 pairs of eyes watching us intently. We are nervous about being judged by an audience and worry about embarrassing ourselves. This makes speaking onstage scary and intimidating. Guess what? Nobody thinks so much about you as *you* do. Nobody cares as much as you think they do.

Your duty as an emcee is achieved when the right message and content of the show comes across. When the message is communicated, people overlook many things and more often won't even realize you made an error. Nobody will remember your pronunciation or grammatical errors except you. You can't be perfect all the time and trying to be perfect and obsessing over it will only make you boring.

After eleven years as a professional emcee, and hosting over 1000 events, there are still moments I get nervous backstage. Even seasoned public speakers face it. No matter how many events you host, you are going to feel the nerves while waiting for the show to begin. In this chapter, I will show you ways to face your fears, and techniques to use before and during your stint onstage.

Be cautious of speeding

When you are nervous onstage you often tend to speak at a faster pace to mask how you feel. When you are rushing as you speak, it is difficult to find the right words at certain moments, leading your mind to go blank so that you don't know what to say next. This will cause you to aimlessly ramble and say things you did not intend to. Therefore, speak at a moderate pace. Make a conscious effort to control your speed and be aware of the words your thoughts are leading to. This will give you time to think about what to say next. Also, when you speak at a moderate pace, it's easier for all the people in the audience to follow what you are saying, making you a good communicator.

Practice

I was once at the airport, waiting to board my flight to host an event in a different city. So engrossed was I in reading and revising the script that I missed my flight to the event. This is the only time I regret rehearsing too much.

The only way to get better at speaking in front of a big crowd is through deliberate practice. There is no secret sauce. The reason most people forget what to say and "go blank" onstage is because they haven't put in enough practice.

Obsessively practice your script as many times as you can, unless you have a plane to board in the next thirty minutes! Repeatedly going through your script and recollecting the message will make the highlights stick. When you have read and registered the content meticulously, you will feel confident about improvising and adding your unique style when presenting onstage. I underline the keywords on my script that I don't want to miss. This way, even if I go blank onstage, I can swiftly look at my script for the highlighted keyword and recollect what next to say.

Well begun is half done

Thirty minutes before my event, I only focus on the opening segment. Because once you get the opening right, you have set the pace. During the opening, your audience, clients, and organizers are glued to your introduction of the event. The opening is most crucial to the emcee because the audience wants to believe the event is worth their time and, from the perspective of an organizer, an event well begun is half done. So double your effort to make the welcome and opening of the show memorable.

When your show has had a delightful start, you will feel a sense of calm, and naturally gain oodles of confidence to be your best self on-stage in the upcoming segments.

Remove distractions

Choose something comfortable to wear. Wear neat, well-fitted clothes that make you feel good. If you feel less confident about wearing a risqué dress or a particular pair of high heels, ditch them for something that makes you confident. Worrying about how you look, and feeling anxious if you are going to trip because of something uncomfortable you are wearing, is a big distraction. Your entire focus and energy should be put into hosting a great show. When you feel comfortable and confident in what you are wearing, you have one less thing to worry about. And that makes a huge difference.

Eat a snack or have a meal one hour before your event. This way you won't feel hungry and distracted when you are onstage.

Switch your phone to silent mode and put it away.

Be there early

If time permits, get on the stage, get hold of the mic, and practice your script before the audience enters the venue. Getting familiar and comfortable with the stage, and associating it with your script, will reduce pre-event jitters.

Get to the event venue at least one hour before the show begins. Meet with the organizers for a final briefing and clarify any doubts you have. Expect some minor changes in the script on the day of the event. Being early will help you adapt to the last--minute changes without feeling flustered, and will eliminate nervousness caused by uncertainty.

Get accustomed to the surroundings and the set-up. There is a whole list of things you need to prep before the event starts. You need to do a thorough sound check of your microphone, figure out how you'll enter and exit from the stage, and where you will be standing onstage. Do a dry-run of your script on the stage before the audience arrives. Rehearsing onstage, in the actual setting of your event, will help you notice and correct errors which you can avoid during the live event. Familiarity with the event set-up will make you more confident. Your physical movement onstage will make the stage seem less intimidating when the actual event starts.

Stay calm before the show begins.

It is good to have a certain amount of nervousness because it makes you alert and keeps you on your toes. It helps you plan and practice better for your stage appearance and compels you to be fully present in the moment. Aim to channel this fear into excitement. When you get the jitters, think of it as an indication to feel excited and be proud of yourself for going out of your comfort zone and exploring your potential.

And go slay some dragons!

5.

Command the stage & look the part

"The difference between ordinary and extraordinary is that little extra."

—Jimmy Johnson
American football player

Your manner, posture, appearance, and attitude matter not only when you are onstage but elsewhere too.

I was an eighteen-year-old trying to fit into the world of large-scale corporate events. The stakes were high. My audience members were on an average twice my age. It did not help that

I was skinny because I frequently found myself trying to convince organizers that though I appeared small and petite, I was capable of commanding a huge audience. I had to overcompensate for my small frame and work extra hard on my stage presence and body language.

Commanding presence

The stage is a few feet elevated above the ground and a few feet distant from the audience. You have to overcome the distance and appear big, and display a presence that will create an impact. The more people are in the audience, the bigger you have to portray yourself onstage. Your energy and enthusiasm should reach the audience, watching and hearing your spiel, fifty meters away from you.

The most important information you communicate onstage is nonverbal.

It comes down to your body language. Like it or not, people judge you in the first few minutes of meeting you. That is why making a good first impression is so significant. When the audience first sees an emcee onstage, they are subconsciously thinking Is this person a friend or a foe?", "Do I want to listen to what this person is saying?", "Should I just check my emails till the bar opens?", etc. So seize the first moments onstage and grab your audience's attention with your presence.

Enter the stage with your

1. back straight
2. shoulders squared
3. chest forward
4. neck straight
5. head held high
6. a smile

When you are nervous you tend to hunch your shoulders and this makes your body appear small. Be conscious about your straight back and shoulders. Be big and be bold.

To help improve and practice my onstage body posture, I do a little exercise called the doorway body-check. Anytime you pass through a door, remind yourself to check your posture. When you open the door, count three-two-one -and imagine a rope holding your back straight, throw your shoulders back and walk through the door with a smile. This will make a big difference in the way you present yourself onstage and offstage when you walk into a meeting or an interview, or a café to meet a date. Through enough practice and muscle memory, it will seem effortless and you will remember to correct your body language when you enter the stage too.

Use gestures

Since I am petite I have to work harder at having a big personality onstage. This is the reason I avoid standing and hosting behind a lectern. I want the audience to be influenced by my emotions and gestures. And I will not be as successful conveying my message behind a wooden box that hides most of me. So to be able to express myself fully and make a visual impact, I prefer standing center stage with nothing blocking me from the audience. The exception to using the lectern is when I have a lot to read, like introductions of speakers or award citations. For instances like these, I need a lectern to spread my notes and stay organized.

Figure 1 & 2 - Being consumed by huge lecterns.

Use your hands and make gestures to appear bigger. Your posture and gestures will add to your authority onstage. The best public speakers use their power sphere[1] efficiently. Picture your power sphere as the area from the top of your eyes, out to the tips of your outstretched arm, down to your

39

belly button and back up to your eyes again.[1] Using hand gestures within the power sphere is a display of confidence and makes the audience perceive you as a leader. Don't let your hands hang below your waist and outside of your power sphere; this can signal a lack of energy and confidence. Don't keep your hands bound onstage. As an emcee, I hold cue cards in my left hand and the mic in my right. When I'm not holding cue cards, and wearing a wireless headset microphone, I bring my hands together and casually wrap my fingers around each other and bring them close to my waist. My elbows are pushed outwards and sideways, and I attain a bigger frame which makes me seem bigger in comparison to if I stood with my hands hanging by my sides.

Do not overdo the hand gestures for the sake of it. Do not try to mimic someone else's gestures. Use gestures as a natural part of your conversation and to enhance your words.

Figure 3 & 4 - Using hand gestures in my power sphere

Figure 4 photo credit – Richard Jeffrey

Figure 5 - Notice my hands are still in the 'power sphere' in spite of
no hand gestures

Photo credit – MJ Jahangir

Find your feet

Movement on stage is necessary to keep your audience engaged. But too much moving around while speaking defeats the purpose. Here are some dos and don'ts regarding footwork on stage.

Dos

- Stand with your feet shoulder-width apart. This posture will give you balance. When you keep your feet together you will not find stability, therefore making it difficult to relax your body.
- Your feet should point towards your audience.
- Moving around the stage will keep the audience from losing interest. Use movement as a tool for transition while you take your audience from one idea to another.

Don'ts

- Don't stand too close to the edge of the stage.
- Don't restlessly sway your body from one side to the other. It's a sign of nervousness. Walking too much, and fidgeting, signals a lack of control and competence.

Figure 6 - my feet are slightly apart to give me stability.
Photo credit – The Red Crab

Show your emotions

Smile and radiate warmth. If there is something more
important than being a competent show host, it is being likable
to your audience. You are a friend to the audience. They like
you and want to be your friend. Your audience and you are
experiencing the event together. Make them feel like you are
one among them.

"Don't be afraid to share your excitement. It will rub off on your audience." - Carmine Gallo

Smile. Pause. Look at your audience and then start speaking. When you smile and speak, your voice will naturally convey warmth and welcome. Audiences react to your non-verbal cues. So if you seem confident and relaxed, you will reassure and comfort them. Energy moves easily between the stage to the crowd. Be enthusiastic. You can choose to be enthusiastic the moment you open your mouth. Even if things go wrong, at least nobody will complain you weren't trying hard.

To engage with your audience, you must let your emotions come across. When you say "I am so excited to be here tonight!", mean it. If you are hosting the launch of an IT product, truly believe it is revolutionary. If you are celebrating a company's recent success, be ecstatic for the team and celebrate with them. Be invested in the ideas you are talking about and involve your audience emotionally.

By just being enthusiastic, you can create a better impact and a greater experience for the audience in comparison to a celebrity emcee who is low on energy and dispassionate.

Maintain eye contact with the audience. It is not possible to make eye contact with each and every individual, so find a friendly face in the audience to make eye contact. There is always at least one kind person in the audience whom you can immediately spot and who is keenly listening to you, smiling, and nodding at what you say. This person is your ally; anytime you want reassurance, just look to your ally. Then turn to the other side of the audience and find another group to engage with.

How to look onstage

"Dress shabbily and they remember the dress, dress impeccably and they remember the person" - Coco Chanel.

Be clever about how you dress for your meetings and events, and how you carry yourself. It seems unfair, but people are making judgments based on how you walk, talk, and look. Superficial aspects matter because organizers are looking for someone who can represent their brand.

You don't need to be a fashionista to be an emcee. By following some classic rules of dressing you can appear put-together and relevant.

Dress for the occasion

Wear what is appropriate for the event. For example, don't wear a leopard print cocktail dress when hosting a business conference for CFOs.

While choosing what to wear, factor in the following:

> ➤ the brand you are representing (is the brand fun and young or traditional and conventional?)
> ➤ the background of the audience (are the attendees young sales and marketing teams or older, business owners?)
> ➤ the venue (is the event indoors, in a banquet hall or outdoors by the beach)

Shoes

Choose shoes that are well fitted and well kept. Because an emcee stands onstage, which is generally at eye level for the seated audience, your footwear will not go unnoticed. Make sure your shoes look neat and clean.

Colors

Bear in mind the backdrop of the stage while choosing what to wear. I avoid wearing black onstage unless specifically requested by the organizer because black absorbs light and wearing all black makes it difficult to compete with a dynamic background. Wear solid colors that pop onstage. My go-to color is red. Wearing red makes me feel like Beyoncé! So find a color or style that wakes your inner Beyoncé and wear more of it.

If you want to know what colors compliment you best, find your skin's undertone. Is it warm, cool, or neutral? If the veins on your wrist look blue, your skin has a cool undertone. If your veins look green, your skin's undertone is warm. Colors like dark blue complement those with cool undertones. Colors like dark green, red, and yellow look beautiful on warm skin tones.

Comfort over everything

Wear outfits that you are comfortable in. Through the entire event, you will be navigating in and out of the stage and sometimes walking among the audience.

Don't try to be overtly sexy. Remember the event is about the brand and what the brand means to the audience. You are not the show-stopper or the major attraction of the event. So, women, stay away from short hemlines and plunging necklines. Men, no matter how many weights you've been lifting, button up your shirt.

Lighting

When testing your mic also check for the lighting onstage before the event starts. Get someone to take photos of you onstage and find the intensity and the color of light that flatters you the most. With the help of the light technician at the venue, get the desired effect. I prefer bright yellow lights instead of white lights for when I am onstage.

Grooming

Learn basic makeup, and hair styling, for those moments you can't find a professional to help you. Makeup and hair tutorials on YouTube are very helpful for learning the basics. Men with facial hair and eccentric hairstyles, groom yourself appropriately when hosting a formal event.

Quality check

Wear outfits that fit you well and are your size. Your clothes shouldn't be ill-fitted or too tight. Do a quality-control check on your clothes before you step onstage. Check if there are any loose threads hanging or if your undergarments are exposed. Whatever you wear, the most crucial aspect is to make sure it is clean, neat, and wrinkle-free.

I predominantly host events in an Indian city where being full-figured is considered appealing and attractive. I might have even lost a few events solely on the basis of physical appearance. This frustrated me so much. After constantly wishing I looked the 'standard', I realized that since these comments were not about my work, I shouldn't let them affect me. The only feedback I will accept and work on is feedback about my hosting skills. Value yourself for who you are. I take a lot of pride in having a successful career filled with many iconic events, in spite of not having conventional looks that the industry in my city desires.

When you are a public personality, people are always going to have an opinion on how you must look. Don't let it affect your game. All that truly matters is that you are healthy, physically and mentally. In a profession which involves interacting with a lot of people, it is necessary to be fit and full of energy. It will take time to accept your unique beauty, but you must begin. When you are an emcee, your skill at communicating the message, command over the audience, stage presence, and attitude take precedence over physical beauty.

(1)Power sphere - Carmine Gallo's Talk Like Ted: The 9 public-speaking secrets of the world's top minds

6.

How to execute and manage a corporate event

"The only way to do great work is to love what you do."

— Steve Jobs

Business magnate and investor

The best part of being an emcee is that each workday is different. Each event you host is unique from the previous one though they have similar goals. In this chapter, I will take you through the different types of corporate events you will be approached for and how you can run the show onstage.

Product launch/ press conference

New brands or new products are launched with a lot of fanfare and aplomb at a launch event. A press conference is organized when a company wants to get particular information out in the media with the aim of leveraging its brand amongst its customers. You could host an event to launch a new shampoo or a car, or announce the launch of a company's specialty service. Through this event, your client expects to get the word out and garner mileage in the industry. This is a popular public relations exercise.

The audience is generally a combination of stakeholders of the company, employees, customers, members from the press and media, journalists, and photographers. With the rise of influencers, bloggers and vloggers, it is common to find them at launch events these days.

Company annual day/ annual get-together

Companies organize a day of fun and entertainment to celebrate the past year and raise a toast to all the successes and achievements. These events boost employee morale. It is one day that brings the entire company together to celebrate. These events can sometimes include a segment of awards, rewarding and recognizing certain teams and individuals. The audience is comprised of employees, stakeholders, and top management, and may include spouses and families of the employees.

Corporate retreat & team building

Companies host retreats or a fun day out for their employees or specific teams. Team- building games are a great way for the employees to have fun together and unwind. As an emcee or game host, your duty is to organize and conduct games, involve everyone in the audience, and get the employees to feel energized. This event involves planning and preparation days in advance. You will need to procure props for your games and customize the games to suit the profile of the audience and include everybody.

IT/ business conference

Conferences are day-long events filled with live sessions, demos, exhibition, and networking. Certain conferences run over a course of two or three days. The attendees are either executives within a company or professionals of a particular industry. Conferences are segmented into multiple sessions headed by speakers. As an emcee, your duty is to guide the attendees through the sessions, introduce the speakers, and make important announcements to help them navigate the different segments of the conference.

How to execute an event

Event execution involves mastering three critical sections:

1. the opening—commencing the event with a bang
2. delivery—taking your audiences from one segment to the next
3. the closing—wrapping the event in style

Opening

The opening of an event is most crucial. It sets the tone for whatever is to follow. It is during this moment that the audience gets acquainted with you. This is when they decide if they should give you their time and attention. You have the opportunity to get your audience excited about the event and curious about all the amazing things that will follow. The opening is when all eyes and ears are on you. Most importantly, the guys spending the dollars—your organizers and clients—are keenly observing you during the opening. So it is wise to put in three times the effort to prepare, practice, and perfect your opening.

Backstage prep

You are all set backstage. Ready to roar. The event attendees are filling up the venue. The event is about to begin in a few minutes.

Make backstage announcements welcoming the audience and informing them that the show will begin shortly. This way the audience is alerted to proceed to their seats. Remind them to put their phones on silent so there are no interruptions during the live event. I always insist on making backstage announcements because I open up and break the barrier in the cozy comforts of backstage versus having to do it onstage. Listening to how I sound gives me a good feeling that everything is in place. I also like to get my audience prepared and anticipating my entry onto the stage.

Before speaking on the mic, drink some water and clear your vocal cords. Listening to a speaker with a dry throat is less desirable. Stay hydrated.

Get the DJ to play upbeat music for your entry onstage. Cue the technician responsible for lights to illuminate the stage or throw a spotlight on you in preparation for your grand entrance.

It's show time!

The goal of your opening is to grab the attention of the audience and commence the event proceedings. Prepare them for what is about to unfold and build curiosity.

- ➢ Walk onstage with confidence, back straight, and chest lifted. Look up, smile, and speak.
- ➢ Greet your audience and welcome them.
- ➢ Unless you are a professional comedian, don't open with a joke. Your joke might fall flat or be taken out of context. Listening to crickets at the end of a one-liner can crush your confidence and derail you.
- ➢ Keep the opening line simple. A bold "Good evening, ladies and gentlemen" gets the job done.
- ➢ Introduce yourself as the event host
- ➢ Your script should cover the following:
    - ○ A brief on what is going to happen through the course of the show
    - ○ A few words about your client's company
    - ○ The company's latest victory/ achievement
    - ○ Acknowledgment of key members in the audience like the chief guest or a VIP or the founder of the company

   o Mentioning and thanking the sponsors (if any)

➢ Build excitement around the event and be an excited spectator yourself. Be a fan!

➢ Don't just talk to the audience, engage with them.

➢ Encourage the audience and nudge them to cheer on, and use them to create an atmosphere of excitement. Create hype from the beginning of the show and get the audience charged up.

To summarise, the opening must be welcoming, informative, succinct, and create curiosity.

Example scripts

Opening script at a healthcare conference

Good Morning, ladies and gentlemen. Welcome to the fifth edition of Zen Healthcare and Wellness 2019.

Today we are here to celebrate health and nurture the community that is invested in the health and well-being of our nation. Over the years, the Zen Healthcare and Wellness conference has played a significant role in increasing efficiency as well as the performance of the industry as a whole. This conference has successfully brought under one roof the country's greatest minds and renowned leaders in healthcare.

My name is Dhwani Rao, and I will be your host for the next two days. The theme for this year's conference is powerful and universal: 'Innovation beyond the lab'. We bring to you over the course of the next two days eminent speakers from the healthcare and wellness sector including doctors, surgeons, government representatives, consultants, and medical technology innovators.

Before we move on to the sessions, here are a few important announcements.

Please switch your phones to silent mode.

Tea, coffee, and refreshments are available throughout the day in halls two and three.

We encourage you to use our event hashtag #InnovationBeyondLab across your social media platforms for sharing live updates of the event.

If you have questions for our session speakers, you can tweet us the question. Our twitter handle is @ZenHealthcareConference.

Our event volunteers are around in case you have further event-related queries.

I would like to take this moment to thank our sponsors for their support. Zen Healthcare and Wellness conference 2018 is powered by GreenPlus in partnership with The Chronicle Network. We would also like to thank our supporting partners Lotus Healthcare, Pearson Hardman, IFTC Bank, and Zoomit Communication.

Now, to kick start the conference this year, may I invite onstage the dynamic Ms. Jessica Pearson, President of Zen Healthcare and Wellness Conference, to welcome you all.

Opening script at a smartphone launch event

Good Evening, ladies & gentlemen! On behalf of S Mobiles, I would like to welcome you to celebrate the launch of yet another superstar from the Star Note family—the all new, super powerful, Star Note 10. My name is Dhwani Rao and I am thrilled to be your host for the evening.

As we all know, the Star Note has a legacy of tech innovation for the "go-getters". The Star Note series is powerful and nothing short of sheer brilliance.

The latest from S Mobiles comes packed with oodles of processing capability, the new Star pen, all day battery, and expandable memory up to five terabytes.

The Star Note 10 will be unveiled to us live for the first time on this very stage, but before that, it is my absolute privilege to welcome onstage the man of the hour, Nick Berry, CEO, S Mobiles to say a few words.

Delivery

You have created an exciting opening. You need to help sustain audience attention and keep them curious as you take them through speeches and other entertainment. Managing the event onstage as an emcee requires you to ensure the show appears seamless to those watching.

- ➢ Have the copy of the event agenda with you and be ready for the next segment.
- ➢ Invite on stage the key persons, speaker or performer. Make sure you have their name with the designation right.
- ➢ If you have any doubt about how to pronounce a name, check with the organizer or, better, ask the speaker how it is supposed to be pronounced.
- ➢ When you introduce a speaker onstage, your script should include details of the speaker's achievements, about the topic they are about to address, and how the speaker's knowledge is going to help the audience.

Giving a great introduction for a speaker will boost their impact on the audience.

➤ Thank the speaker at the end of their session. Be attentive and listen to what was said in the presentation. Pick a nugget of information or a quotable quote from the speech and re-iterate it when you thank the speaker.

➤ If you are inviting a performer onstage, talk about the art they will display. Say a few words about the theme of the performance and invite the individual or team by their name.

➤ Maintain excitement and energy throughout the event, but do not scream or shout into the mic in an attempt to sound energetic.

Be concise and to the point, to help you keep up with the schedule, time, and tempo. The focus is always on the speakers or the proceedings of the event. You are only guiding the attendees from one segment to the next.

Example scripts
Introducing a speaker at a corporate event

We at Zotware love to challenge the norm and disrupt the market. Our next speaker is one of the most sought after investors in the country. His passion for innovation has transformed his business into the country's leading cloud-based software company. I'm pleased to welcome Mr. Mike Ross, Founder CEO, TechForce, to our annual celebrations. He is a bonafide product superstar. I know we have many in the audience who are fans of his latest bestseller, Experiment Iterate. Today Mr. Ross will talk to us about 'Going after value proposition'. With a round of applause, please join me in welcoming the dynamic Mr. Mike Ross!

Thanking the speaker

Thank you, Mr. Ross, for sharing with us valuable insights on market fit, marketing, and scaling up. The value-bombs shared by you are sure to add tremendous value to team Zotware. Your journey of building TechForce from the ground up is truly an inspiration to tech-entrepreneurs across the country. May I invite onstage Ms. Rachel Zane, Head, Marketing, Zotware to present a memento to our session speaker as a token of our gratitude. Ladies and gentlemen, give it up for Mr. Mike Ross.

Closing

It's now time to draw things to a close. Here is how you can end the event on a high note.

➢ A good closing should highlight the success and achievements of the event.

➢ You should recognize all those involved in making the show a success.

➢ Thank the chief guest, speakers, performers, and the sponsors.

➢ Thank the audience for being part of the event.

➢ Make relevant announcements and reminders like requesting delegates to submit their feedback form or reminding them to collect their gift bag or sponsored gift from the registration desk.

➢ Invite and direct the audience to dinner or the bar.

➢ If there is a DJ scheduled to perform post-event, introduce the DJ and a nice touch would be to go into the crowd and get the audience on the dance floor.

In summary, you have to thank everyone involved and end on a positive note. Keep the entire talk brief because you don't want to come between the audience and the bar.

Example script
Closing a Tech conference

They say all good things must come to an end and so does the fourth edition of Sports App Creators' Summit. I would like to take this moment to thank all our speakers for joining us, sharing valuable insights, and inspiring all of us. A big shout out to our sponsors who have helped make this summit a success. I would like to thank our title sponsor NBS Sports, our co-sponsor Codeline Apps, and our venue partner The Dome. Before I let you go, may I request you to kindly fill out the feedback form and drop it with our volunteers at the registration desk. We love to hear your feedback. I would like to welcome you to more networking over dinner. The bar is open. Cocktails and dinner are being served in the pre-functional area. It's time for me to sign off. My name is Dhwani Rao and I'm hoping to see all of you in the next edition of Sports App Creators' Summit. Have a great evening!

Closing a corporate annual day

With that, ladies and gentlemen, it's a wrap. Once again can we give it up for all our amazing and talented singers who kept us entertained through the evening? I would like to thank all of you, our most valuable employees and teams, for joining us and celebrating Bloom Media's Fifth Anniversary. The night is young and, in true Bloom Media style, we are going to party the night away. Ladies and gentlemen, make some noise for DJ Nash. See you on the dance floor.

7.

Wedding events— preparation & execution

"Make each day your masterpiece."

— John Wooden
American basketball player

Hosting weddings can feel intimidating because it is a momentous occasion for two individuals and their families. In my experience, weddings are the most fluid events to host. Even with a structured schedule and itinerary in place weeks before the event, changes and time delays are inevitable. Be prepared to adapt as the event proceeds. Your goal as a wedding emcee is to get the attendees, family, and friends to enjoy this special day with the bride and groom.

When a couple gets in touch with an emcee for their wedding, they already have a vision. Since weddings are more personal and private in comparison to a corporate event, meet with the bride and groom days or weeks ahead of the event. Though couples have a vision for their reception party, they might not know what exactly they need from the emcee on their big day. Use this meeting to understand your role and brainstorm with them. Sharing your ideas and experiences will add a lot of value and credibility.

Get to know the couple

- Be interested in their story. Ask the couple how they met. Are they childhood sweethearts? Did a cousin play cupid? Did they meet in college? Be excited for their big day! You can incorporate these cute details in your script.
- Understand the cultural background of the couple.
- Which part of the wedding festivities will you be emceeing? Is it a reception or a celebration that is unique to their tradition?

- Do they imagine their reception to have a lot of singing and dancing? Do they want an intimate reception with a few speeches followed by dancing?
- What do they want the emcee to fulfil?
- These questions will help you get a sense of what the couple wants, and will give you direction.

Planning

- How far is the couple in the planning process? Find out details of what is being planned.
- If you are organizing fun games, research and plan the games.
- Are there other entertainers performing at the event? Are relatives or friends of the couple performing a dance? Get the list of entertainers, singers, and dancers who are scheduled to perform onstage.
- Who is making the speeches? Get their names and how they are related to the bride and groom.

Be organized

- Start making an event flow. Write down everything. Add every detail starting with the bride and groom's entry, the speeches, performances, cake cutting, opening the dance floor, and dinner. Make sure you have all the names right. Get the agenda approved by the couple. This way there are no surprises.

- Create an endearing introduction to welcome the bride and groom.

- Prepare fun introductions to introduce friends and relatives who are making speeches.

- Always be prepared for more. In case you need fillers, have a wedding game for the couple up your sleeve. If there are any delays in the event, be ready to engage with the audience. Have a couple of quirky and cute questions to ask about the couple to the friends and family in the audience.

On the day of the event

- Your role as an emcee is to give directions to the audience. You are running the show and only taking the audience from one segment to the next.

- Whenever you speak, keep it brief. Let the bride and groom shine and let the family and friends do most of the talking about the newlyweds.

- Get to know the other vendors of the event like the DJ, photographer, videographer, band etc. so you can cue them when required. Brief them on the event itinerary. Knowing what is going to happen next will help the photographer capture all the fun moments and help the DJ play the most suitable track.

- Know who the speakers and performers are and keep them organized. If a friend or relative is scheduled to speak, make sure they are around before you invite them to speak onstage.

- In the end, get the couple, their families, and the rest of the guests on the dance floor.

While you are emceeing at weddings, keep the focus entirely on the couple and their romantic story. Your duty is to make everything about the couple. It's the biggest celebration of their lives. So shower all attention on them and create delightful memories for them. Since weddings are intimate celebrations, be involved and celebrate this big day like a member of their family.

Be mentally prepared for a lot of changes on the day of the event. Consider yourself as the person responsible to smooth things out. All that matters is how you made the bride and groom feel on their big day. So go out there and celebrate the newlyweds.

8.

Managing glitches and difficult audiences

"To avoid criticism, say nothing, do nothing, and be nothing."
—Aristotle
Philosopher

Even a well-planned event can have a technical malfunction and unexpected delays, and even the most admired emcee can be faced with a difficult audience. Since the emcee is the thread that connects and brings the entire event together, you must be ready and prepared for damage control.

Delay in the event

Delays can be caused when the first speaker or the chief guest of the event is yet to arrive. Attendees get antsy while waiting for the event to begin. So as the face of the event, get on the stage, greet your audience, and inform them about the anticipated delay. Let them know how long it will take for the show to begin and sincerely apologize on behalf of the organizers.

A delay between the sequences of an event is commonplace. This could be caused by a speaker who just realized his live demo is broken and is fixing it frantically, or performers dealing with an audio hitch backstage. This is when an emcee is key as they will prevent the audience from knowing about all the chaos. Here is what I do to fill the gap and ease the wrinkle.

- I use the time to thank the sponsors, talk about the event's dedicated hashtag for social media, remind the audience to fill their feedback form, and make other house announcements.
- I walk into where the audience is seated, interact with them and get them talking.

- If I foresee a delay of over five minutes, I conduct an ice breaker game and, if the event is informal, I get members in the audience to sing or shake a leg and get the rest of the audience cheer for them.

Technical glitches

Kanye West's mic failed during his performance at the Pan Am games' closing ceremony in Toronto. He tossed it in the air and stormed offstage.

Emcees face technical glitches like a blackout, a mic failing mid-speech, and an unflattering audio. But we are not Kanye and we shouldn't display anger or displeasure onstage. Also, microphones are delicate and expensive, so you don't want to break them. You can reduce the probability of audio glitches by completing a thorough sound check before the event begins. Work with the technician behind the audio console and choose the right levels. Arrive early. Test your mic onstage at least thirty minutes before your guests walk inside the venue. Walk through the seating arrangements to make sure the sound has no interference or feedback in any part of the room. But sometimes in spite of an elaborate sound check, you could still face this problem. For moments like these, have a back-up mic close by, and calmly exchange your mic and continue from where you left off.

During an unexpected blackout onstage, stay calm. When the lights are back, apologize to the audience for the glitch and move on. Audiences are more forgiving than you think.

Difficult audience members

Emcees thrive on validation from the audience. All presenters want to be liked by their viewers. But unfortunately, sometimes we are given a hard-to-please crowd. Don't let it throw you off-balance; just remind yourself that, to be a professional, you need to stay focused and believe in yourself and your skills.

Unruly members in the audience

You will come across a person or two in the audience who will mumble comments on the proceedings and laugh with their peers. These antics derail the speakers onstage, although all the audience wants is some harmless fun. Don't take it personally and don't feel intimidated. Depending on the event you are hosting, there are two ways to handle this. Focus on the content you have to say, deliver it, and get done. Unruly behavior in the audience is momentary. The next time you are back onstage, they will have run out of things to say. At less formal events, I give the unruly member what he needs: attention! I start a conversation with him, ask for his name, and engage in a fun conversation. As a by-product, the audience will find you likable and friendly and feel encouraged to be nice to you. After this interaction, I turn my focus back on the content and my duty as the master of ceremony.

Bored and tired spectators

At business functions, your audience members probably had a long day at work and are here at the event to fulfil an employee obligation. You might find some attendees slouching, yawning, and looking bored. Don't let their body language bring your spirit down. You have the power to get the audience with you. So bring your best confident posture onstage, and project energy and enthusiasm so they can mimic your body language. Reassure the audience that you are going to bring them a great show. You can inspire, entice, and fascinate the audience but you can't force everybody to listen to everything you say. Accept this fact and be patient. Your job is to create curiosity around the event. Don't let non-verbal cues like yawning or a bored look bring your enthusiasm down. They are not a reflection on your public speaking skills, but simply means the person is tired. Sustain your confidence and enthusiasm through your entire time onstage.

Low turnout

From my experience, sales conferences that have their agents as attendees generally have a slow start. The room eventually gets filled only in the second or third session. But the show must go on. We can't wait indefinitely for the hall to fill up. When an event has a low turnout, the attendees are sitting alone, by themselves, in different parts of the hall. They are spread out. You will notice them staring at the empty spaces between the rows of seats, contemplating why they came. Make announcements and request all of the attendees to move forward and be seated in the rows in the front. Gather them to a smaller area in the front. This way the audience is packed densely like a group and no-one is left feeling lonely in a huge, almost empty hall. Also, the speakers will thank you for this later.

9.

What organizers look for in an emcee

"Loyalty is not won by being first. It is won by being best."

—Stefan Persson

Business magnate

Through my career as an emcee, I have met so many people of diverse backgrounds, from different industries, different nationalities, and holding different positions of seniority in their company. After over 1000 events I still meet clients and organizers who surprise me with some of their requirements. I was once asked to "Welcome the audience and do some mimicry". After an awkward pause, I explained to my client that I was an emcee and not a stand-up comic.

Organizers are not looking for an emcee that can double as a stand-up comedian, a celebrity impersonator, or a singer. If you are approached by someone asking you to do anything more than host an event onstage, politely decline.

So, what are companies looking for in an emcee? Here is what will get organizers knocking at your door.

- **Energy & enthusiasm.** Your clients expect you to bring great energy that inspires and excites the audience. They expect the emcee to keep the audience engaged throughout the event. A skilled emcee is someone who can create and sustain the audience interest in the event. Companies want an emcee who their audience will like.

- **Communication.** Organizers want to have on-board an emcee who has excellent verbal communication skills and good command over the vernacular language. Inappropriate language or expletives onstage or offstage are a big no-no. Keep your personal, political, religious opinions private as you are representing a company and it could conflict with its beliefs. This will affect not just the event, but also reduce your credibility as an emcee. Be courteous and formal in all your communication onstage and off.

- **Command a presence.** Companies choose an emcee that can represent their brand and display the values that the brand believes in. They want an emcee that looks the part. An organizer of a business conference will look for an emcee that can hold their own in a room filled with senior professionals. Companies want someone smart enough to grasp the concept behind their event and convey the message in an appealing manner onstage. Organizers need emcees that have authority and can command a presence. They want their emcee to stand out and direct the audience through the entirety of the show. They want to hire someone who is capable of running the show seamlessly onstage.

- **Be a partner.** Contribute to the discussions. Be an active member of the creative process. Take the initiative to understand the company's mission and the event's goal. Be the brand you are representing onstage. Offer to create the script if it is not prepared in-house. Be open to working with the materials provided.

Three years ago I hosted the annual day celebrations for a division of Bosch. After speeches and fun games, it was time to present the annual team awards. I announced the winners and the winning team gathered in huge numbers onstage. I noticed the backstage was short staffed. There were only two ladies from the HR team struggling to carry the prizes from the wings to the presenter. It was taking too much time and there was a hold-up. I moved away from my lectern between announcing each segment of awards and helped carry the gifts to expedite. It might seem like a small gesture, but sometimes all it takes is how much you are invested in the success of the event. We are in the people business and small acts like these can create a positive reaction. My clients now love me for being a team player and I have been hosting their annual day events since, three years in a row. Teamwork makes the dream work!

- **Punctuality.** If you want to be taken seriously at work, be on time. Organizers want to work with professionals who respect their time. Being a few minutes early is always a good idea. On the day of the event, organizers have hundreds of things to check on their list and fix. So having you there and knowing you are prepared and all set gives respite to an organizer.

- **Integrity.** Do not divulge any confidential, client, or organizer information. If there is any conflict of interest, you have to be honest and upfront about it.
- **Respect.** Maintain a respectful attitude with everybody you work with. The event industry is often stressful as it is running live. Hence the stakes are high. Don't be disrespectful or lash out onstage or offstage even during stressful times.
- **Take responsibility.** Do what needs to be done. Take accountability when you fail. Be honest when things go wrong and work out a solution to overcome it. Nobody is perfect and people are forgiving when you own up to your mistakes.
- **Commitment.** Companies look for someone who can deliver what they promise. When you are at the event, be committed to its success. Make that your greatest and most important goal of the day. This attitude will make the overall experience of working with you pleasant and enjoyable.

A long-term work relationship between an emcee and an organizer has more to it than great public speaking skills. This is a business. Event organizers and corporate clients expect a high level of professionalism. This is paramount if you intend to last for years in this field and become a sought-after emcee in your city.

While working on perfecting your public speaking and event hosting skills, also work on developing personal credibility. After all, personal credibility is the foundation for any professional success.

10.

Brand building; create a hot brand with personal marketing

"All of us need to understand the importance of branding. We are CEOs of our own companies: Me Inc. To be in business today, our most important job is to be head marketer for the brand called You."

—Tom Peters

Business author and speaker

I was once getting briefed for an event by an organizer and she quoted my lines from an event footage she'd watched on my website. The organizer used the video as a reference and asked me to replicate my script. I was so flattered that someone quoted me. The organizer had keenly observed my style, language, and flair through my videos online which convinced her I was suitable for her upcoming event.

A strong personal brand can give you an edge and differentiate you from your contemporaries. With the power of the internet and the rise of social media, we have the privilege to create a personal brand and it is easier than ever before. Creating your own personal brand is about creating your best first impression.

Personal branding is bigger than any branding right now. Take for example Elon Musk. He has 26.6 million followers on Twitter while his company Tesla, has only 3.7 million followers.

A few years ago, talking about your competence or skill in your craft used to be considered bragging. We grew up being told, "Don't blow your own trumpet." But now personal branding is very crucial for being known in your field and it helps you to consistently find work. Personal branding is not bragging because you are telling people you are capable of a service they are looking for. In fact, you are helping them easily find a service they need.

Imagine you are hosting a party at home. You know you will have at least seventy-five guests over. You organize and plan every detail like food, music, wine, etc. On the day of your party, nobody arrives. Nobody turns up because you did not send out invitations to anyone. How do you expect them to come to your party when they did not even know about it? [2]

This is what lack of personal branding can do to your emceeing career. If you want organizers knocking on your door and booking you for their events, you have to invite them into your world and show them what you do.

The importance of personal branding

I just got booked by a leading interior design brand for their upcoming event. During my chat with my event organizer, I learned that they were impressed that I had hosted the launch of Construction Architecture and Interiors Expo, a renowned industry expo. If I had not uploaded the expo's video on my website, my organizers would not have known I hosted a prestigious event in their industry. Showcasing my work and showing what I do gave me an edge and helped me bag the gig. If I didn't promote my work, most organizers would not know the scale and size of the events, or the range of industries, I have worked in.

In my personal experience, the top two avenues that result in most event opportunities are:

- ✓ event videos
- ✓ word of mouth

I started my website in 2013, six years after I started emceeing and almost three years before my competitors caught up and created their websites. What initially started as a vanity project for me, today brings in most of my new clients. My website is simple and straightforward. It has event-centric photographs, a short introduction to what I do, videos from my events, and a page to get in touch with me.

When creating your website, focus on what matters. Superficial aspects are important but don't spend your time and money on portfolio shots for your website. Your clients don't want a model or an Instagram influencer; they are looking for an emcee. What is most essential is to show potential clients that you are capable of hosting a show onstage. So what better way than showing video footage of your work? If you are just starting your career as an emcee, don't get caught up in trying to put a website together. It is not a prerequisite to be an emcee. You don't need to have it at the beginning of your career.

As an emcee, your prospective clients are all around you. Your client could be an event professional, a twenty-eight-year-old bride, or someone you went to high school with. I get a lot of inquiries on Facebook from people within my network, friends of people I know, and also people outside of my network. People are watching your work through the social media platforms and they will approach you when they see the right fit. Your immediate social circle or network might not be your clients, but they have the power to influence other people, and to suggest you to the right people. So, make them a fan and give them reasons to promote you in their circles. Even if you have a small social media following of 500, they could become loyal influencers and open gates to work opportunities.

Here is how you can get started with creating your hot personal brand.

Find your personality and style

Know who you are and what your style is. Be authentic. When you are a beginner, it is difficult because you feel like you are all over the place. We try to emulate others who are successful. To understand yourself better, try hosting different kinds of events, and be seen by as many people as you can. Gain some confidence. Observe and notice the style you are best at. What kind of events do you enjoying hosting the most? This is your niche. I host all kinds of events, but my niche is hosting conferences. I truly enjoy hosting them and I am good at it.

Document your work

However small (or big) your gig is, document it. Get photographs clicked and video footages of your performance onstage. Hire a professional or get a friend to accompany you to your event and shoot videos of it. Always let your organizers know that you would like to shoot snippets of the event. Some companies might not approve of sharing the video on a public platform because of confidentiality reasons.

Use the photos and videos from your events

- in your profile
- to create a showreel
- to make posts on your social media pages
- to upload on YouTube
- on your website

When your clients appreciate an event well done, request them to write a testimonial or get a recorded video testimonial. This can be used in your profile and your website.

Scrub & clean

Do a thorough audit of your social media profiles. Remove and delete any post from the past that makes you seem unprofessional. Your social media profile should reflect your personality which is charming, cordial, and professional. Delete any extreme political or religious views which might deter potential clients and decision makers. While looking for an emcee, your clients want somebody to reflect their company's values and ethics. They want to make sure the host is warm, gracious, and smart.

Update

Fully update your social media accounts. Fill in all the relevant information and mention what you do. Add your email ID or a phone number to help potential clients get in touch with you in an instant. If you have a website, create a 'contact' page to help organizers reach you.

Aesthetics

Your profile picture must have your face visible and identifiable. Get a good image of yourself holding a microphone and speaking onstage for your profile picture. This will create a befitting first impression of you. By doing so, the people you interact with, friends and family, will immediately know you are open for business in this career.

Get creative

Creating content is not as easy as it seems. Being creative does not come naturally to everyone. Follow people you look up to in the event industry and be inspired by the content they share. Observe them. Looking at what they share will help you generate ideas.

Be regular

Share content on a regular basis. Like it or not, if you are not promoting your work, people think you aren't doing any. Always create a buzz around your stage persona. I share around three to five social media updates a week, which includes pictures of me onstage, backstage selfies, details of my events, and the companies I work with. Find a schedule that works for you. Create a repository of images and videos. There are several apps and tools available to help you plan and schedule your social media activity.

Keep it positive

Whatever you are posting, let it be positive, uplifting, and fun because you are in the business of making people have a good time. So radiate the same philosophy in your online persona too.

Contribute

Join online and offline groups and forums related to the event industry in your city. Contribute to the conversation. Make yourself seen and heard.

Carry business cards

A business card is a great marketing tool. Print a batch of cards with your name on them. Add a title that resonates with you the most: emcee, M.C., event host, corporate event host, or master of ceremonies. Mention the best way to get in touch with you: a phone number and/or email ID and/or a website. At the events you host, you will be approached by prospective clients wanting to speak to you about their upcoming events. Hand them your business card so you can have a detailed discussion at a convenient time later.

Do yourself a favor, do your business a favor, and get the message about your skills out.

(2) Kimberley R. Barker, MLIS, University of Virginia in her Coursera course - Introduction to personal branding

11.

Having a mentor

"Mentors are important and I don't think anybody makes it in the world without some form of mentorship."

—*Maya Angelou*

Poet

Since I started working at a young age, my mother, Madhumathi Rao, played 'momager' to me. In my initial couple of years, I went to her to discuss everything work-related, including money matters and how I should charge, what I should wear, what kind of events to pick and what events to turn down. She was the Kris Jenner to my Kim Kardashian—always telling me I was doing amazing. I give my mother full credit for motivating me to turn my public speaking hobby to my full-time career. I was able to believe in my skill and value myself. We all need that cheerleader in our life and we also need a leveler. I went to my mother, who had no professional experience onstage because, remember, the one time I asked advice from an emcee all I got was flaky "Be yourself" advice, which was useless and led to nowhere.

Fortunately, we now live in a time where there are more people ready to help and see others grow. Having a mentor and grooming a mentee have become popular and we can access advice from a real expert who has the knowledge and wisdom and is willing to help us on this journey.

As an independent artist and as someone running your own business, it is exciting to do it alone and on your terms. You will have great ideas, but the reality is you might find yourself direction-less, not knowing how to go beyond a certain point and how to take your emceeing career further. It takes some mentoring to give you that nudge into the big league.

A mentor in your life will help you prioritize and streamline this process, helping you look at the bigger picture as you work towards your goal.

I've had several mentors in my life. They have helped me with career advice and shaped my biggest career decisions. You need that one person who is in touch with your goals, who inspires you, believes in your talent, helps you get better at your craft, motivates you to be the best emcee you want to be, and thereby helps your career grow.

When I started out ten years ago, things were completely different from how they are now. The event industry was much smaller and the who's-who noticed the new kid on the block. I was winging it. I took each day and each event as it came and did everything my way. I surprised myself with the career I built. But a thriving profitable career like this should not be an accident. The event industry has grown much bigger and gotten better over the last ten years. It is a thirty billion dollar industry worldwide, and event professionals are fighting a cut-throat competition. This is not a career where you want to 'wing it' as I did because there is a replacement waiting to take over the moment you slip. You need to be savvy, be in the right place at the right time, and make strategic decisions at all times. Today, public speaking and hosting onstage are more than just soft skills. They bring hard dollars. Therefore you need a mentor to give you knowledge and perspective so you can learn faster and not miss out on the opportunities at hand.

A mentor can see through your weaknesses and where there is room for improvement. Mentors help you polish your skills. They can help you set goals as an emcee, even the ones you are too afraid to dream of. They can find your potential and help create your overall persona on and off stage.

Lots of emcees diversify over a period in their career. A mentor can be a sounding board for your ideas; someone who can advise you on the initiatives you desire to take, and keep you grounded.

A mentor who is an established emcee can connect you to the right people in the industry. Mentors can open the gateway to vetted, well-known organizers. These connections would otherwise take a lot of time to grow and build organically. Anybody who is willing to share and trust you with their network is hard to find. So this is a gold mine you should value sincerely.

When starting my career, I made a lot of mistakes and I wish I knew then certain things that only experience taught me. In the hyper-connected world we live in, you make one mistake and you have lost your opportunity to a replacement. Every mistake is a very expensive one. Right now, we have so much information around us and people willing to collaborate.

Always remember, asking for help is a clever thing to do and not a sign of weakness. It is a sign of intelligence that you are choosing human knowledge and guidance to improve and benefit your career.

12.

How to charge, and fee negotiation

"Making money is art and working is art and good business is the best art."

—*Andy Warhol*

Artist

After graduating with a in chemical engineering, I took up emceeing full-time. My relatives were so disappointed and felt sorry for me. They couldn't understand why an engineering graduate would let go of a well-paying job in the IT industry. The -twenty-one-year-old me thought I would sound arrogant if I told them how much emceeing paid. So I would just nod whenever they "empathized" with me for my choice of career.

To all those asking how much we get paid for an event, a competent emcee can charge anywhere between $200 to $5000 for an event in 2019.

People ask me why emcees charge so much when an event is sometimes only an hour long. When demand outweighs supply, there is a price to pay. Apart from paying for the emcee's hosting services, an organizer is paying a premium to book an emcee for a particular day, when they could be hosting an event elsewhere. The more the demand for an emcee, the higher the remuneration.

This fee also compensates for the years of practice, experience, and expertise, for the stress that comes with managing the stage during the show, for the pre-event preparation involved, and for the unique skill to make the event more engaging, lively, interesting, and entertaining to the audience.

Setting a price for your services as an emcee is a crucial and sometimes difficult business decision.

HOW TO BECOME AN EMCEE

Your charge is based on a combination of these factors:

- The value and benefits you provide as a stage host.
- How competent you are as an emcee.
- What fee your contemporaries in the industry charge.
- Whether you are famous, a television personality, a radio jockey, or an actress. Whether you can add star power to the show.
- The client's perception about how much it's worth to have an emcee who can entertain the audience.

The good news is there is a great deal of flexibility in terms of altering your fee. But the bad news is there is no formula which you can use to arrive at the ideal and appropriate fee.

Competitor's price

Speak to the other emcees in your city and know how much they charge. Compare your experience and expertise with your contemporaries and see for yourself where you stand. The downside of charging based on competitors' prices is that you are letting competition dictate the rules.

Reducing your price just to override competition will do more harm than good. In the long run, an influx of this strategy could lead to organizers reducing the emcee budget of future events. This will have consequences for the entire emcee community.

In my earlier years, following a few successful events, I asked for more than what organizers were offering me at that time. I believed in the quality I provided. I didn't focus on what the going price was. I made my own rules and I only took up events that paid what I thought I deserved. This strategy worked for me. So use competitors' pricing only to be aware of where the market stands. Use it as a guideline. Don't be consumed by it.

Client's perception

Talk to a few people from the event industry in your city. Get a fair idea of how frequently events are organized. Find how many event companies and wedding planners operate in your city. This is a good indicator of how big the event and wedding business is in your region. Get an insight into how often these events hire an emcee.

While negotiating your first few gigs ask the organizer, "What are you willing to pay?" Remember, the organizers have already allocated certain dollars for every significant element of the event. When the organizer shares with you their approved budget, it is up to you to decide if you want to take up the event for the said budget. At least for an initial couple of events, gauge the industry by how much they are willing to pay for your services and your expertise. By your fifth event, you will have gained more confidence and understanding of the value you provide through the work you do.

From then on, when asked about your fee, be bold, take chances, and quote what you believe you deserve.

Provide value

Give your client value for money. As an emcee, you are committed to elevating the event. Be honest about your experience, proficiency, and competence, and charge accordingly.

Charge differently

I charge more for business conferences that last through the day as opposed to a press conference that is only an hour long. My charges are flexible with organizers I regularly work with.

When you are asked for a quote, understand what the event is. Charge your fee based on the type of the event and the hours you are required. Charge differently for repeat business, for the organizers who hire you frequently. Repeat clients must be highly valued since they typically require minimal additional effort to retain. All you need to do is be consistently good in your work.

Increasing your fee

As a freelancer, you can dictate how much you want to be paid for your time and service. Your fee can be raised from time to time. If you notice your competitors increasing their fee, it is a good time to think about doing so yourself. Raise it in increments.

I have only two rules for you as I wrap this chapter :-don't swindle anyone, and make money.

Always remember you are offering a valuable service. Know your worth! Believe you are worth every dollar you are charging. Believe in the business you are running. Create your pricing strategy.

It is a free market. You decide what you deserve to be paid.

Happy Pricing!

The emcee checklists

Since you are the face of the event, it is critical that you know about the event inside and out. It is your responsibility to make everything look seamless to the audience in spite of all the chaos that happens behind the scenes.

This checklist will help you stay organized. Here is a list of things you need to know and do.

Checklist before the event

- ✓ Request a confirmation email from your organizer.
- ✓ Draw up a contract and invoice and exchange it with the organizer.
- ✓ Block your date on your calendar, so you don't accidentally double-book on a certain date.
- ✓ Find out logistic details like event venue, timings, etc. If the venue is out of your city, discuss your travel and accommodation arrangements.
- ✓ Meet with the organizers or schedule a phone call to get briefed on the event.

Checklist to help you prepare

- ✓ What is the occasion of the event?
- ✓ Know your audience demographic.
- ✓ What is the size of the audience?
- ✓ Get a copy of the event flow.
- ✓ Does the event have a theme?
- ✓ What is the dress code for the event?
- ✓ Do you have the names and introduction for the speakers and chief guest?
- ✓ What are the recurring announcements that need to be made through the event? At what frequency should the announcements repeat?
- ✓ Find out if the event has a dedicated hashtag and make it part of your script to remind your audience.
- ✓ If you are hosting an award ceremony receive details on
    - o the categories of awards
    - o recipients of the awards
    - o name and designation of the presenter of the awards
- ✓ Be prepared for a few audience engagement activities (relevant to the profile of the attendees) in case you need to fill time.

✓ Is there is a celebrity, movie star, or sports personality making an appearance? Create a short and relevant introduction to the star.

✓ Create a script and highlight the important points.

✓ Practice and rehearse your script.

✓ Get a good night's rest before your big show so you can be your best on the event day.

Checklist for the day of the event

✓ Do voice exercises backstage, so your voice opens up and doesn't crack mid-sentence.

✓ Do a sound check on the microphones you will be using. You need to check how your mic sounds from the stage. If you are likely to interact with the audience, walk around the venue and check your mic.

✓ Meet with your organizers one hour prior to the event and finalize the flow of events. Update yourself of any changes. Make sure you completely understand what is going to happen from the start to finish.

✓ Keep the event schedule and script with you at all times.

✓ Practice the right way to pronounce the names of the speakers. Familiarize yourself with the name of the event and the name of the company you are hosting the show for.

✓ Meet with the speakers and performers and ask them how they would like to be introduced.

✓ If the first speaker is running late, prepare ways to fill the time. Think of what you will be doing as filler until your speaker is ready.

✓ Have a meal two hours before your event so you are not hungry and distracted when you are onstage.

✓ Create content for your personal branding. Get someone to take photos during your performance onstage.

✓ Check your appearance, if your clothes and hair are in place.

✓ Stay hydrated. Drink lots of water and keep your vocals hydrated.

✓ Put your phone on silent and disconnect from your phone to avoid any distraction during your event.

✓ Collect yourself and be calm. Stay in your designated side of the wing backstage so you are accessible anytime an organizer wants to get in touch with you.

Note from the author

Recent studies and research have shown that our brains are constantly growing and changing throughout our lives. Doing something repeatedly exercises our brains which naturally makes us better at it. This applies to everything, including learning a musical instrument, writing, or public speaking; the more you practice, the better you get. Our brains are muscles that develops with practice and repetition. So keep at it, continue to practice.

When you do something unconventional and different, there will be a lot of people with opinions on how you should do it. Some will say you talk too loudly, some will say you don't talk loudly enough. I have even had a person find fault with something as inconsequential as my eye make-up at an event. Being in a creative field puts you in a position where people feel free to critique your work. Remember, most of them are projecting their insecurities and failed dreams. You have to cut out the noise, and focus on doing what you believe is the best for you. One of the best pieces of advice I have ever been given is: "Don't take criticism from people you wouldn't ever go to for advice."

Be unapologetic about wanting to turn your passion to profit. When I started writing this book, I had so many doubts and I felt like an imposter. Even after eleven years as a successful emcee in the city, I felt like I did not qualify to write about emceeing. I had to constantly block these self-limiting thoughts and work hard to see my dreams to fruition. You will be faced with the "imposter syndrome" when you begin your career as an emcee. You will have doubts about your capabilities and if you deserve to be paid for this. Remember, all successful emcees started on their first event as a newbie. Stop waiting for the perfect time to start.

What if things work out? What if all your hard work, learning, and practice pays off? I am so excited for you as you begin your journey onstage. I wish you all the success in your career, and the courage and confidence to fulfil your dreams and goals. I hope you become the amazing emcee every event deserves.

Love
Dhwani

About Dhwani Rao

Dhwani Rao is an emcee and a corporate event host. After starting her career at seventeen, she has gone on to become a celebrated and sought-after emcee in India.

With a decade of experience, Dhwani has hosted events for some of the most powerful brands in the world including Microsoft, Toyota, Amazon, Samsung, Cisco, HSBC, and IBM. She has worked for events in diverse sectors including technology, manufacturing, energy, healthcare, telecommunications, retail, education, and at diplomatic events for the Government of India.

Having hosted over 1000 events across the country, she is now frequently booked to host business conferences, product launch events, and award ceremonies.

Dhwani's skill set lies in bringing any event to life with her enthusiasm, and delivering the target message to the audience.

Dhwani is fluent in four languages and is a chemical engineering graduate. Dhwani gets show-ready while listening to her special Beyonce playlist.

Hang out with her on Instagram @DhwaniRao. To find out more about her work, head to dhwanirao.com.